RELATIONSHIP TIPS FOR
Life Partners

The Secrets of Happy Relationships Series

DR. LAURIE WEISS

Empowerment Systems Books

Relationship Tips for Life Partners
The Secrets of Happy Relationships Series
Dr. Laurie Weiss
© 2019 Laurie Weiss

All rights reserved. No part of this book may be reproduced in any form or by any electronic or mechanical means, including information storage and retrieval systems, without permission in writing from the publisher, except by a reviewer who may quote brief passages in a review.

The author has done her best to present accurate and up-to-date information in this book, but she cannot guarantee that the information is correct or will suit your particular situation.

This book is sold with the understanding that the publisher and the author are not engaged in rendering any legal, medical or any other professional services. If expert assistance is required, the services of a competent professional should be sought.

First published as 124 Tips for Having a Great Relationship

Library of Congress Control Number 2018960330
Paperback 978-1-949400-10-6
Ebook 978-1-949400-11-3
Downloadable audio file 978-1-949400-12-0

Books may be purchased in quantity by contacting the publisher directly at:
Empowerment Systems Books
506 West Davies Way
Littleton, CO 80120 USA
Phone 303.794.5379
LaurieWeiss@EmpowermentSystems.com
www.EmpowermentSystems.com

Cover: Nick Zelinger, www.NZGraphics.com
Interior Design: Istvan Szabo, Ifj.
Family & Relationships / Marriage & Long-Term Relationships / Self-Help

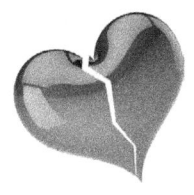

Special Bonus

When:

- You do want to help your partner with a problem.
- You do know how to help with the problem.
- If only your partner would only listen to you, s/he would appreciate how smart you are.
- You feel frustrated because you are only trying to help.

You need *How to Both Win the "Yeah But…" Game.*

The secret is to learn how to avoid this deadly relationship trap and empower your partner instead. It's easier said than done—until you know how! Claim your copy and learn this important trick right now.

www.BooksbyLaurie.com/win

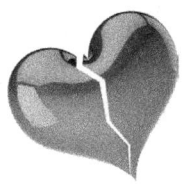

Contents

Special Bonus	3
Introduction	7
Chapter 1: About Relationships	9
Chapter 2: Communication	12
Chapter 3: Difficult Communication	17
Chapter 4: Play	21
Chapter 5: Tasks	24
Chapter 6: Boundaries	27
Chapter 7: Money	31
Chapter 8: Special Occasions	35
Chapter 9: Separateness	38
Chapter 10: Togetherness	40
Chapter 11: Care of Your Partner	44
Chapter 12: Self Care	50
Chapter 13: The Secret to Success	53
Personal Journal	59
Special Bonus Reminder	119
Please Help Me Reach New Readers	121

Acknowledgments	124
About the Author	127
How to Work With Dr. Laurie	130
About the Secrets of Happy Relationships Series	134
Books in the Secrets of Happy Relationships Series	137
Other Books by Laurie Weiss	137
Reconnect to Rescue Your Marriage: Avoid Divorce and Feel Loved Again	141

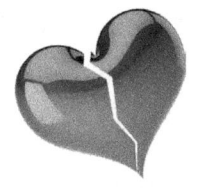

Introduction

Your relationship deserves a chance to grow and enhance your happiness and satisfaction. However, becoming partners in a relationship can be a real challenge.

Most of the forces that surround you conspire against creating a truly co-creative partnership relationship with your chosen life partner. You are taught to compete and give in, to be either one up or one down. You may never have imagined doing things differently and have very little idea of what a different kind of relationship even looks like.

What you do know is that you want something different!

When my husband and I married in 1960 (yes, that's a long time ago) we couldn't even conceive of anything except a traditional marriage. Gradually, while experimenting and practicing our own partnership relationship as psychotherapists, marriage counselors and teachers, we learned.

We learned that relationships either grow or stagnate. And we learned that, like us, our clients have many misconceptions about how relationships really work. These tips are many of the things I found myself saying over and over again to my clients in order to counter those destructive beliefs and help them evolve their own relationships.

These tips come from that learning, and from a practice that spans over four decades. They have been used by thousands of people to move toward true partnership relationships. Use them any way you like – and if you want to know more about how this project developed, read my story in the acknowledgment section at the end of this book.

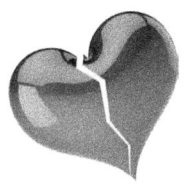

Chapter 1:
About Relationships

1. Expect differences. We tend to choose relationships because our partner is different and then spend all our time trying to get him or her to change and be exactly like us.

2. Change the behavior in yourself that you don't like in your partner. It is all too easy to ignore things you don't like about yourself, and instead, pay attention to how annoyed you are that your partner does those very same things. This is called projection.

3. Expect the closeness and distance you experience with your partner to vary from hour to hour, day to day, and season to season. People experience enough closeness much as they experience enough food—any more leads to discomfort. We all have different capacities.

4. Understand that the experiences you had as children influence how you respond to each other now. Barely remembered traumatic events may make you or your partner hypersensitive to events that someone else would consider trivial.

5. Accept that differences are just that—differences. When you take the position that you are right and your partner is wrong, nobody wins.

6. Vary your responses. Don't expect to always give in or to always have it your own way. Getting stuck in any position drains the energy from a relationship.

Relationship Tips for Life Partners

7. Learn from your experience. Notice what works and what usually receives a negative reaction from your partner. Do what works and stop doing what does not work.

8. Expect to "fall out of love" with your partner. Being "in love" is temporary insanity that lasts long enough for nature to get babies started. A mature loving relationship is better and takes time to develop.

9. Create a mature, loving relationship by using the ideas in this booklet. Loving relationships do not just happen—creating them is a rewarding and worthwhile challenge.

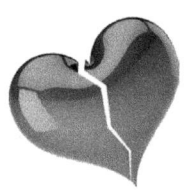

Chapter 2:
Communication

10. Be courteous. Your partner deserves the same respectful communication you would give a stranger or a business associate.

11. Ask your partner for what you want. Contrary to popular belief, your partner cannot and should not read your mind. Asking increases the odds of getting what you want. Be specific.

Relationship Tips for Life Partners

12. Tell the truth about what you do and do not like or want. Trying to be agreeable when you really do not agree leads to confusion and resentment.

13. Use a rating system to let your partner know how strongly you like or dislike something. Knowing whether something is a "1" or a "10" makes it easier for your partner to decide how to respond to you.

14. Say "Maybe" when you are not sure about something. Give a time when you will provide an answer and keep your commitment.

15. Express your appreciation when your partner does something that pleases you. People love being acknowledged and behavior that is acknowledged is usually repeated.

16. Keep agreements you make with your partner. Keeping agreements builds trust, which is the basis of almost everything important.

17. Renegotiate any agreements that you find you can't (or don't want to) keep. If you intend to change an agreement, let your partner know at the earliest opportunity, even if you feel uncomfortable about doing so.

18. Use feeling words like sad, mad, glad, and scared to describe emotions. Saying "I feel (sad or glad)..." is better than saying "I feel THAT YOU..." Once you say the phrase "that you," you stop describing feelings and switch to a judgment you are about to lay on your partner.

19. Ask if your partner has time to listen to a long story before launching into it. It also helps to tell your

partner, in advance, why you're telling the story. Then s/he can prepare appropriate sympathy, suggestions, or questions while listening to you.

20. Listen carefully to what your partner says. Ask direct questions until you really understand what your partner is telling you. Attentive listening is often the greatest gift you can give another person.

21. Allow your partner time to think about the answer to your question and to answer at his or her own speed. Leaving a few seconds of quiet may seem uncomfortable at first but may allow time for important thoughts to surface and be expressed.

22. Find out whether your partner wants your help in solving a problem before you jump in and offer suggestions. Some people just want a sympathetic listener and will feel insulted if you try to help.

23. Ask what kind of help your partner wants before taking action. Your partner may surprise you by asking you to do something you would not think of on your own.

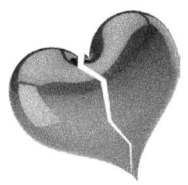

Chapter 3:
Difficult Communication

24. Discuss problems as soon as you recognize their existence. Do not pretend things are OK when they are not—resentments that build up over time are harder to manage than the original problems.

25. Figure out what you want your partner to do differently when you are angry and communicate specifically what s/he can do to satisfy you. Most people don't want to hear about anger because they think there is nothing they can do to fix it.

26. Warn your partner when you are about to change the rules and do things differently. If you have always hung up the clothes s/he left around, say that you will no longer do that task.

27. Speak in sentences or, at most, paragraphs instead of pages during a difficult conversation. Your partner will only remember the last sentence or two you say and forget the beginning of a long speech.

28. Paraphrase your partner's words when you are having a difficult conversation and ask if you understood the words correctly. Just saying "I understand" is usually not telling the truth: you probably don't.

29. Add your own thoughts to the conversation only after your partner acknowledges that you understand. This slows down a difficult conversation and makes it less likely that you will say things that you will later regret.

Relationship Tips for Life Partners

30. Create conversations by phone, text or even email instead of face to face when you keep getting stuck in the same old patterns. It is often easier to stick to discussing information when you can't react to the expressions on each other's faces.

31. Confront behavior you consider dangerous or destructive. Describe your own feelings about the situation. "I feel scared when the car moves this fast," instead of "You're driving too fast."

32. Request that your partner change behavior that causes you a problem. If you ask for what you want, you are more likely (but not certain) to get it than if you keep quiet and stay annoyed.

33. Explain how a change you are requesting will solve a problem for you, without implying that s/he is wrong

or bad for doing what upsets you. After all, s/he may honestly believe that making beds is a waste of time.

34. Decide what you will do when you partner persists in behavior you have requested that s/he change. Tell your partner about your decision. The next time that behavior occurs, do what you said you would do—even if you are scared.

35. Admit your mistakes—even if you don't like the way your partner confronts you about them. It is tempting to defend yourself by attacking your partner, but if you do, you both lose in the long run.

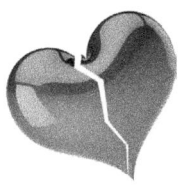

Chapter 4: Play

36. Play together in silly ways. Blow bubbles; finger paint with chocolate pudding on the kitchen table and lick it off; splash each other; sing.

37. Enjoy touching each other in both sexual and non-sexual ways. Enjoy is the important word—it means you must communicate about what is pleasurable and what is not.

38. Laugh together. Share the jokes or cartoons that make you grin, rent a funny video, or remember the stories about funny things (especially in retrospect) you've experienced together.

39. Schedule time to play together. Keep a list of activities you each consider fun. Take turns choosing an item from the list and do it.

40. Walk, hike, or plant flowers together. Being outdoors, even to do "work," makes most people feel happy.

41. Take a mini-vacation. Go away for the weekend, or for an hour or two, with minimal planning, just because it seems like a good idea.

42. Organize the activities *you* are most interested in doing. If your partner agrees to accompany you to a

concert or sporting event you particularly want to attend, you get the tickets.

43. Challenge your partner to resolve a problem with a squirt bottle duel at ten paces. If the situation is really serious, try aerosol whipped cream (at three paces) instead.

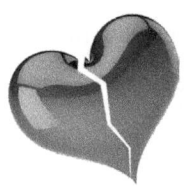

Chapter 5:
Tasks

44. Negotiate about tasks. Avoid sex role stereotypes. Divide chores based on individual preferences and skills.

45. Hire someone to do the chores you both hate—or do them together. Start by looking at the things that never seem to get done, probably because neither of you wants to do them.

46. Work together on something hard that will feel great when it's done, like removing a dead tree stump or tearing down an old fence or wall. The sense of accomplishment helps you feel connected to each other.

47. Make clear agreements about which of you will do which parts of a complicated task, like arranging a vacation. Check each item off your joint list as it is completed. Posting the list on the bathroom mirror or the refrigerator door works well.

48. Avoid emergency shopping trips. Keep a running shopping list. The person who takes the last item from storage should note that it needs replacement.

49. Inform your partner as soon as possible if you will not be doing a task that s/he expects you to do. This avoids

unpleasant surprises and lets you solve the problem of what to do about the undone task together.

50. Share a routine task one of you would normally do alone. Spend the time talking together and enjoying each other's company.

51. Occasionally do a task that your partner doesn't expect you to do. Let your partner be pleasantly surprised that s/he doesn't need to prepare dinner or mow the lawn.

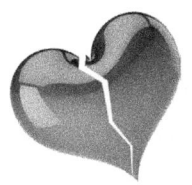

Chapter 6: Boundaries

52. Give up control of "your" kitchen if you want your partner's help. So what if you have to look for something that is not in its proper place—it probably is not very far away, and you can ask if you get desperate.

53. Give up control of "your" tools if you do not want to do all repairs yourself. If things get scattered, discuss boundaries that will suit both of you.

54. Protect what is important to you. If you have a cherished collection that is yours alone, or a private journal, or tools you use for your own work, it's fine to set clear boundaries and not allow your partner access to them.

55. Respect your partner's boundaries. If you are curious, ask why it's important to your partner to keep some special thing private, but do not insist on seeing or using it.

56. Name the movie *you* would like to see, or the restaurant *you* like best, before you ask your partner's preference. That way you avoid being angry because your partner did not read your mind.

57. Negotiate by first asking the reason for your partner's preference. You may think your partner wants a

particular kind of food, when s/he really likes the atmosphere or service at a particular restaurant.

58. Make clear agreements about how to play with other people when you and your partner enjoy very different activities. If your partner hates the music or movies you love most, which other people is it OK for you to enjoy them with? How frequently? With how much advance notice?

59. Let your partner know when you are distressed instead of dumping anger that belongs to someone else into your relationship. If someone is mean to you, tell your partner instead of passing on the meanness.

60. Share the power and the decision making. Avoid the resentment that comes when one is burdened with responsibility and the other resents being told what to do.

61. Forgo retaliation. If you think your partner is preoccupied and ignoring you, look at the ways you are ignoring your partner and change your own behavior. This works for any behavior you don't like.

62. Go to obedience school training with your dog. You must learn to communicate clearly about boundaries when you work with animals.

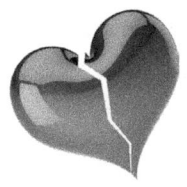

Chapter 7: Money

63. Talk about money. Discuss where it comes from and where it goes, and why.

64. Keep track of money regularly. Balance your checkbook(s), know your credit card balance(s), and be aware of large expenses and plan for them.

65. Use a computer system such as Quicken to track where your money is coming from and going to. You can use

this information to make informed decisions about how to allocate or budget your resources.

66. Decide on an equitable way to share resources and expenses. This can be especially tricky if you have very different income levels. Keep talking until you reach agreement.

67. Renegotiate financial agreements as your circumstances change. Changing paychecks, changing personal and family needs, and changing priorities all call for renegotiation.

68. Consider having his, hers, and ours accounts, and decide which expenses will be paid from which account. Most people feel happier and more empowered when they don't need to account to anyone else about their personal spending.

69. Create shared financial goals. Be sure you discuss and agree on priorities. If one of you thinks your savings are for a great vacation and the other expects to use them to invest for financial independence, you are headed for trouble.

70. Consult a financial advisor if your financial situation is complex, especially if one of you has substantially more resources than the other or if you are creating a blended family. Professional advice can help resolve money anxieties.

71. Forgo retaliation about money. If your partner spends money in a way that upsets you, discuss the problem instead of going out and spending to get even with your partner.

72. Spend less money than you make. Use the extra to build a reserve. Relieving money-related stress gives you energy for the things that really matter.

73. Share responsibility for financial decisions. Two heads are better than one, and when you are both responsible, neither of you is to blame if your results don't meet your expectations.

74. Accumulate a team of professional advisors. Find health, legal, financial, and other resources before you actually need them.

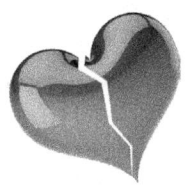

Chapter 8:
Special Occasions

75. Celebrate birthdays, anniversaries, and holidays that are important to your partner, even if they are not important to you. Your partner's comfort will ultimately contribute to your own happiness.

76. Request that your partner celebrate special events in your life in the way that is most meaningful to you. Emphasize exactly what you want and how you want it, or your partner may not understand your needs.

77. Create your own holiday traditions. You come from different families with different traditions. Choose what is most meaningful from each and combine them into something that will satisfy both of you.

78. Clarify the obligations and priorities you each feel about visits with your extended families. Relationships with in-laws may be challenging for either of you.

79. Offer special support to your partner during challenging family visits. Some people need more support in relating to their own parents and siblings than to their partner's family.

80. Develop your own special occasions. They can be to celebrate something you have experienced together or just because.

81. Listen for hints about what gifts your partner would love to receive. Pay attention to what excites or delights your partner and use that information when you shop.

82. Give gifts that your partner has indicated that s/he wants or needs instead of what you believe s/he wants or needs. You can give other gifts, too, but first paying attention to your partner avoids disappointment.

83. Create a mutually loving way to communicate when one of you receives a gift that doesn't "work" for you. Have this important conversation before, not after, a gift-giving occasion.

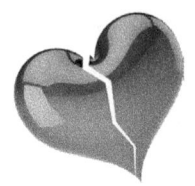

Chapter 9:
Separateness

84. Keep your individuality while building your relationship. Two becoming one is an outmoded notion—it really means that each of you becomes half the person you were and is guaranteed to lead to resentment.

85. Remember that you are a complete person and so is your partner. You are neither responsible for nor capable of completing each other.

86. Encourage your partner to find ways to do things s/he loves, even if you don't share the same interest. You don't have to do those things if they are uncomfortable for you. There is no rule that says you must do everything together.

87. Encourage your partner to grow and develop in his/her own way. This does *not* mean to chase your spouse around the house with a self-help book.

88. Listen even when you disagree. Understanding your partner's position about something is not the same as agreeing with it.

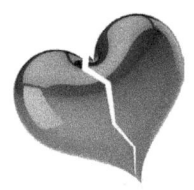

Chapter 10: Togetherness

89. Spend time working on your relationship as well as living in the relationship. Good relationships do not just happen—they need to be watered and weeded, just like a garden.

90. Live your lives now. Don't wait until you get a better job, move to a new house, have a baby, or until the kids leave home—live now!

Relationship Tips for Life Partners

91. Attend classes and workshops together. Going through an adult education catalog and choosing what you would like to learn together is a good way to tune in to your partner's interests.

92. Talk to each other for at least ten minutes a day about your daily successes, dreams, hopes, fears, and disappointments. These important things sometimes get lost in the challenge of managing the logistics of complicated lives.

93. Fill out magazine questionnaires about your interests or personality, pretending that you are your partner. Compare notes and see if you know your partner as well as you think you do.

94. Discuss your personal and joint priorities. Take time together periodically to make sure you're on track.

95. Do little things for each other, even if it's not a special occasion. Bring home flowers for no reason. Give your spouse a gift certificate for a round of golf, a facial, or a special favor from you, just because.

96. Expect major life changes to impact your relationship. Having a baby, losing a job, getting a new job, illness, death of a parent, retirement, etc., may create a need to renegotiate almost everything you thought was settled.

97. Avoid blaming your partner for a problem in your relationship. Address all problems as if you both contribute to them. You do!

98. Feed each other. If only one of you has cooking skills, or only one of you has time to cook, reverse roles occasionally anyway. Feeding can be as simple as bringing your partner a cup of tea or offering to go out for ice cream.

Relationship Tips for Life Partners

99. Play for favors. If either of you needs forgiveness for something you have done or failed to do, agree on a favor you can do that will heal the resentment.

100. Support your partner in contributing to your community. Contributing time, money, or energy to causes you both believe in will cement your relationship.

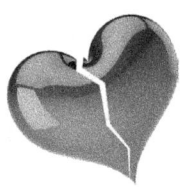

Chapter 11:
Care of Your Partner

101. Remind your partner about the wonderful qualities s/he brings to your relationship. Remember what attracted you in the first place—personality, creativity, warmth, appearance, strength, feistiness, whatever.

102. Thank your partner for the routine things s/he does to make your life more pleasant. Does s/he wake you with a kiss and a cup of coffee or do the driving late at night when you're both tired?—remember to say thanks.

Relationship Tips for Life Partners

103. Surprise your partner with a special treat. It does not need to involve money—a massage, a library book by a favorite author, a walk to see some flowers that are just blooming or taping a special TV program can count as much as an expensive gift.

104. Catch your partner doing something right and acknowledge it. It's easy to complain when something is wrong, but we tend to expect things to go right. Your recognition will be appreciated.

105. Avoid disappointing your partner. Don't promise to do things just because your partner wants you to, when you suspect you won't be able to keep the promise.

106. Say aloud the nice things you think about your partner. Just because you think your partner already

knows you care does not mean s/he would not like to hear about it.

107. Hug your partner frequently—not just when you want to get sexy. Touch is an important way that people use to know that they are loved.

108. Find out what makes your partner feel loved and do it frequently. Some people need time, others need touch, others need words of affirmation, others love gifts, and others feel loved when you do things for them.

109. Encourage your partner to get professional help if you think s/he needs it. Offer to go along if that seems helpful.

Relationship Tips for Life Partners

110. Support your partner by listening to him or her express feelings of sadness about a loss. You probably can't fix the loss or solve the problem, but just being close will help the healing process.

111. Estimate your time commitments accurately. Tell your partner what time you are most likely to be home instead of when you *hope* you'll be home (if traffic is not too heavy and you make all the lights.)

112. Compliment your partner in public, complain only in private. Be sure to include what you wish your partner would do differently as part of your complain.

113. If you have a problem with your partner, talk about it together. If you need advice about how to discuss a problem, ask a trusted advisor privately.

114. Say, "I'm sorry" when you accidentally hurt your partner instead of explaining why s/he should not be hurt because you didn't mean to cause any harm. Sometimes that's all it takes to fix the problem.

115. Give your partner the greatest gift you can give another person. Listen to him or her with your full attention.

116. Honor your partner's report of how s/he feels. Insisting that s/he does or should feel differently about anything is like saying you understand your partner better than s/he understands him/herself. You don't!

117. Empower your partner to seek his or her own happiness. It is not your responsibility, nor is it within your power, to make your partner happy.

118. Avoid doing anything that you know, from past experience, will cause your partner pain. If you feel you must do it anyway for some reason, discuss it ahead of time with your partner, and see if, working together, you can find a way to minimize the pain.

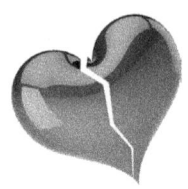

Chapter 12: Self Care

119. Do whatever makes you feel vibrant and alive, even if you need to do it alone. When you feel vibrant and alive, you are attractive to your partner and to others.

120. Take responsibility for arranging to get what you need and want in your life. This is not your partner's job, although s/he may be happy to help you in your quest if you communicate it clearly and request help.

Relationship Tips for Life Partners

121. Make sure you ask for the acknowledgment you want from your partner. If your partner doesn't notice your new haircut or the amount of work you did to arrange an event, say something instead of waiting for your strokes.

122. Get help when you need it. If you feel stuck, depressed, or upset for more than a couple of weeks, talk to someone (a counselor, coach, or other trained professional) who can help.

123. Consider carefully whether or not to do something your partner wants you to do when you don't want to do it. Sometimes doing something you do not especially want to do for your partner costs you very little in time or inconvenience and is very important to your partner. Sometimes it's very expensive emotionally.

124. Trust your hunches enough to check them out. If you suspect that something is wrong, for either of you, talk about it. Everyone makes up stories about small bits of barely noticed information—stories that may or may not be true.

125. Make taking good care of yourself a priority. In airplanes, you are reminded to put on your own oxygen mask first, before you assist others. In relationships, taking care of yourself regularly enables you to fully engage with your partner.

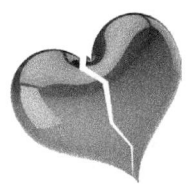

Chapter 13:
The Secret to Success

This is about the Secret you probably already know and wish you didn't!

It's that no matter how well you understand something, it won't work until you put it into practice. Putting these tips into practice is simple but may not be easy.

Certainly, no important new habit is easy to *remember to practice*. Habit easily takes over and leads us to revert to our old ways of doing things.

I want you to be successful! So, to increase the odds of you actually incorporating these new practices into your life, I have created the following guided journal pages that you can use to record your adventures with this material.

Your personal journal is for 30 days. That is because it takes about a month to make a new habit pattern into a regular part of your life.

One of my teachers once insisted that I do something for 30 days *without any interruptions* and start the count over again after a single missed day. That's a great way to increase motivation but it can be frustrating. It took me about 90 days to complete 30 days without interruption. Of course, by that time, my new habit was a solid part of my life.

You certainly don't need to be *that* committed to finding more love and joy in your life. You can if you want to though. You decide what will work best for you.

Keeping a record of what you do has also been shown to increase the likelihood of it getting done more frequently. Many years ago scientific research showed that when the number of packages put into shipping containers was counted, many more were actually put into shipping containers than when the packages were not tracked.

Do make notes to keep track of what you are doing. It will make a huge difference.

Writing about your journey will also make it easier for you to see how easy it really can be to create the relationship you want so much to have.

Each daily journal sheet includes a few lines to record your plans, results and feelings. That's all it takes.

I have included a way to record your emotions because emotions are critically important and often ignored when you take action to change your habits. Emotions are temporary responses that often change once they are acknowledged.

Here are instructions as well as examples of things you might record.

My Plan

Each day choose the section of this book that seems most important to you and your relationship at that moment. I like to do this at the end of my day, so I can review my day and plan for tomorrow.

For example, if you are feeling frustrated about communicating with your partner about something, choose the Communication or Difficult Communication section. If you need to take better care of yourself, choose the Self-Care section.

Read that section and choose one tip to focus on for the day. Record your tip number and a few words to remind you about what it is when you reread this journal.

Today I chose to focus on Tip # __ because: (chose something that concerns you now) example: we had an argument about money yesterday.

I will experiment by: (choose something you can do to carry out your experiment) example: balance my checkbook and list and add up all outstanding credit card balances.

Because: (write the reason for your choice) example: I want to really know where I/we stand financially.

Right now, I feel: (notice and record your emotions, even if they are not very strong, such as sad, mad, glad, scared or some combination of those feelings) example: a little scared about my choice

About 24 hours later, after you have done your experiment, complete this section.

My Results

When I did this experiment, I noticed: example: that balancing my checkbook was easier than I expected it to be.

Right now, I feel: (sad, mad, glad, scared or some variation or combination of those feelings) example: happy about my experience today.

Congratulate yourself!

Decide what you are going to do next and start the process again on the next page of your journal.

Do keep track; it will make a huge difference.

Note: My ideas of activities to put these tips into practice are in another book in this series, *Being Happy Together: What To Do to Keep Love Alive.*

Personal Journal

Day 1

My Plan

Today I chose to focus on Tip # ___ because: _____

_____

_____

I will experiment by: _____

_____

_____

Because: _____

_____

_____

Right now, I feel: _____

_____

_____

Do your experiment.

My Results

When I did this experiment, I noticed: _____

_____

_____

_____

Right now, I feel: _____

_____

_____

_____

Congratulate yourself!

Decide what you are going to do next and start the process again on the next page of your journal.

Day 2

My Plan

Today I chose to focus on Tip # ___ because: _____

_____

_____

I will experiment by: _____

_____

_____

Because: _____

_____

_____

Right now, I feel: _____

_____

_____

Do your experiment.

My Results

When I did this experiment, I noticed: _____

_____

_____

_____

Right now, I feel: _____

_____

_____

_____

Congratulate yourself!

Decide what you are going to do next and start the process again on the next page of your journal.

Day 3

My Plan

Today I chose to focus on Tip # __ because: _____

_____

_____

I will experiment by: _____

_____

_____

Because: _____

_____

_____

Right now, I feel: _____

_____

_____

Do your experiment.

My Results

When I did this experiment, I noticed: _____

_____

_____

_____

Right now, I feel: _____

_____

_____

_____

Congratulate yourself!

Decide what you are going to do next and start the process again on the next page of your journal.

Day 4

My Plan

Today I chose to focus on Tip # ___ because: _____

_____

_____

I will experiment by: _____

_____

_____

Because: _____

_____

_____

Right now, I feel: _____

_____

_____

Do your experiment.

My Results

When I did this experiment, I noticed: _____

_____

_____

_____

Right now, I feel: _____

_____

_____

_____

Congratulate yourself!

Decide what you are going to do next and start the process again on the next page of your journal.

Day 5

My Plan

Today I chose to focus on Tip # ___ because: _____

_____

_____

I will experiment by: _____

_____

_____

Because: _____

_____

_____

Right now, I feel: _____

_____

_____

Do your experiment.

My Results

When I did this experiment, I noticed: _____

_____

_____

_____

Right now, I feel: _____

_____

_____

_____

Congratulate yourself!

Decide what you are going to do next and start the process again on the next page of your journal.

Day 6

My Plan

Today I chose to focus on Tip # __ because: _____

_____

_____

I will experiment by: _____

_____

_____

Because: _____

_____

_____

Right now, I feel: _____

_____

_____

Do your experiment.

My Results

When I did this experiment, I noticed: _____

_____

_____

_____

Right now, I feel: _____

_____

_____

_____

Congratulate yourself!

Decide what you are going to do next and start the process again on the next page of your journal.

Day 7

My Plan

Today I chose to focus on Tip # __ because: _____

_____

_____

I will experiment by: _____

_____

_____

Because: _____

_____

_____

Right now, I feel: _____

_____

_____

Do your experiment.

My Results

When I did this experiment, I noticed: _____

_____

_____

_____

Right now, I feel: _____

_____

_____

_____

Congratulate yourself!

Decide what you are going to do next and start the process again on the next page of your journal.

Day 8

My Plan

Today I chose to focus on Tip # ___ because: _____

_____

_____

I will experiment by: _____

_____

_____

Because: _____

_____

_____

Right now, I feel: _____

_____

_____

Do your experiment.

My Results

When I did this experiment, I noticed: _____

_____

_____

_____

Right now, I feel: _____

_____

_____

_____

Congratulate yourself!

Decide what you are going to do next and start the process again on the next page of your journal.

Day 9

My Plan

Today I chose to focus on Tip # ___ because: _____

_____

_____

I will experiment by: _____

_____

_____

Because: _____

_____

_____

Right now, I feel: _____

_____

_____

Do your experiment.

My Results

When I did this experiment, I noticed: _____

_____

_____

_____

Right now, I feel: _____

_____

_____

_____

Congratulate yourself!

Decide what you are going to do next and start the process again on the next page of your journal.

Day 10

My Plan

Today I chose to focus on Tip # ___ because: _____

_____

I will experiment by: _____

_____

Because: _____

_____

Right now, I feel: _____

_____

Do your experiment.

My Results

When I did this experiment, I noticed: _____

_____

_____

_____

Right now, I feel: _____

_____

_____

_____

Congratulate yourself!

Decide what you are going to do next and start the process again on the next page of your journal.

Day 11

My Plan

Today I chose to focus on Tip # ___ because: _____

_____

_____

I will experiment by: _____

_____

_____

Because: _____

_____

_____

Right now, I feel: _____

_____

_____

Do your experiment.

My Results

When I did this experiment, I noticed: _____

_____

_____

_____

Right now, I feel: _____

_____

_____

_____

Congratulate yourself!

Decide what you are going to do next and start the process again on the next page of your journal.

Day 12

My Plan

Today I chose to focus on Tip # ___ because: _____

_____

_____

I will experiment by: _____

_____

_____

Because: _____

_____

_____

Right now, I feel: _____

_____

_____

Do your experiment.

My Results

When I did this experiment, I noticed: _____

_____

_____

_____

Right now, I feel: _____

_____

_____

_____

Congratulate yourself!

Decide what you are going to do next and start the process again on the next page of your journal.

Day 13

My Plan

Today I chose to focus on Tip # ___ because: _____

_____

_____

I will experiment by: _____

_____

_____

Because: _____

_____

_____

Right now, I feel: _____

_____

_____

Do your experiment.

My Results

When I did this experiment, I noticed: _____

_____

_____

_____

Right now, I feel: _____

_____

_____

_____

Congratulate yourself!

Decide what you are going to do next and start the process again on the next page of your journal.

Day 14

My Plan

Today I chose to focus on Tip # __ because: _____

_____

_____

I will experiment by: _____

_____

_____

Because: _____

_____

_____

Right now, I feel: _____

_____

_____

Do your experiment.

My Results

When I did this experiment, I noticed: _____

_____

_____

_____

Right now, I feel: _____

_____

_____

_____

Congratulate yourself!

Decide what you are going to do next and start the process again on the next page of your journal.

Day 15

My Plan

Today I chose to focus on Tip # __ because: _____

_____

_____

I will experiment by: _____

_____

_____

Because: _____

_____

_____

Right now, I feel: _____

_____

_____

Do your experiment.

My Results

When I did this experiment, I noticed: _____

_____

_____

_____

Right now, I feel: _____

_____

_____

_____

Congratulate yourself!

Decide what you are going to do next and start the process again on the next page of your journal.

Day 16

My Plan

Today I chose to focus on Tip # ___ because: _____

_____

_____

I will experiment by: _____

_____

_____

Because: _____

_____

_____

Right now, I feel: _____

_____

_____

Do your experiment.

My Results

When I did this experiment, I noticed: _____

_____

_____

_____

Right now, I feel: _____

_____

_____

_____

Congratulate yourself!

Decide what you are going to do next and start the process again on the next page of your journal.

Day 17

My Plan

Today I chose to focus on Tip # ___ because: _____

_____

_____

I will experiment by: _____

_____

_____

Because: _____

_____

_____

Right now, I feel: _____

_____

_____

Do your experiment.

My Results

When I did this experiment, I noticed: _____

_____

_____

_____

Right now, I feel: _____

_____

_____

_____

Congratulate yourself!

Decide what you are going to do next and start the process again on the next page of your journal.

Day 18

My Plan

Today I chose to focus on Tip # ___ because: _____

_____

I will experiment by: _____

_____

_____

Because: _____

_____

_____

Right now, I feel: _____

_____

_____

Do your experiment.

My Results

When I did this experiment, I noticed: _____

_____

_____

_____

Right now, I feel: _____

_____

_____

_____

Congratulate yourself!

Decide what you are going to do next and start the process again on the next page of your journal.

Day 19

My Plan

Today I chose to focus on Tip # ___ because: _____

_____

_____

I will experiment by: _____

_____

_____

Because: _____

_____

_____

Right now, I feel: _____

_____

_____

Do your experiment.

My Results

When I did this experiment, I noticed: _____

_____

_____

_____

Right now, I feel: _____

_____

_____

_____

Congratulate yourself!

Decide what you are going to do next and start the process again on the next page of your journal.

Day 20

My Plan

Today I chose to focus on Tip # ___ because: _____

_____

_____

I will experiment by: _____

_____

_____

Because: _____

_____

_____

Right now, I feel: _____

_____

_____

Do your experiment.

My Results

When I did this experiment, I noticed: _____

_____

_____

_____

Right now, I feel: _____

_____

_____

_____

Congratulate yourself!

Decide what you are going to do next and start the process again on the next page of your journal.

Day 21

My Plan

Today I chose to focus on Tip # ___ because: _____

_____

_____

I will experiment by: _____

_____

_____

Because: _____

_____

_____

Right now, I feel: _____

_____

_____

Do your experiment.

My Results

When I did this experiment, I noticed: _____

_____

_____

_____

Right now, I feel: _____

_____

_____

_____

Congratulate yourself!

Decide what you are going to do next and start the process again on the next page of your journal.

Day 22

My Plan

Today I chose to focus on Tip # __ because: _____

_____

_____

I will experiment by: _____

_____

_____

Because: _____

_____

_____

Right now, I feel: _____

_____

_____

Do your experiment.

My Results

When I did this experiment, I noticed: _____

_____

_____

_____

Right now, I feel: _____

_____

_____

_____

Congratulate yourself!

Decide what you are going to do next and start the process again on the next page of your journal.

Day 23

My Plan

Today I chose to focus on Tip # __ because: _____

_____

_____

I will experiment by: _____

_____

_____

Because: _____

_____

_____

Right now, I feel: _____

_____

_____

Do your experiment.

My Results

When I did this experiment, I noticed: _____

_____

_____

_____

Right now, I feel: _____

_____

_____

_____

Congratulate yourself!

Decide what you are going to do next and start the process again on the next page of your journal.

Day 24

My Plan

Today I chose to focus on Tip # ___ because: _____

_____

_____

I will experiment by: _____

_____

_____

Because: _____

_____

_____

Right now, I feel: _____

_____

_____

Do your experiment.

My Results

When I did this experiment, I noticed: _____

_____

_____

_____

Right now, I feel: _____

_____

_____

_____

Congratulate yourself!

Decide what you are going to do next and start the process again on the next page of your journal.

Day 25

My Plan

Today I chose to focus on Tip # ___ because: _____

_____

_____

I will experiment by: _____

_____

_____

Because: _____

_____

_____

Right now, I feel: _____

_____

_____

Do your experiment.

My Results

When I did this experiment, I noticed: _____

_____

_____

_____

Right now, I feel: _____

_____

_____

_____

Congratulate yourself!

Decide what you are going to do next and start the process again on the next page of your journal.

Day 26

My Plan

Today I chose to focus on Tip # __ because: _____

_____

_____

I will experiment by: _____

_____

_____

Because: _____

_____

_____

Right now, I feel: _____

_____

_____

Do your experiment.

My Results

When I did this experiment, I noticed: _____

_____

_____

_____

Right now, I feel: _____

_____

_____

_____

Congratulate yourself!

Decide what you are going to do next and start the process again on the next page of your journal.

Day 27

My Plan

Today I chose to focus on Tip # ___ because: _____

_____

_____

I will experiment by: _____

_____

_____

Because: _____

_____

_____

Right now, I feel: _____

_____

_____

Do your experiment.

My Results

When I did this experiment, I noticed: _____

_____

_____

_____

Right now, I feel: _____

_____

_____

_____

Congratulate yourself!

Decide what you are going to do next and start the process again on the next page of your journal.

Day 28

My Plan

Today I chose to focus on Tip # ___ because: _____

_____

_____

I will experiment by: _____

_____

_____

Because: _____

_____

_____

Right now, I feel: _____

_____

_____

Do your experiment.

My Results

When I did this experiment, I noticed: _____

_____

_____

_____

Right now, I feel: _____

_____

_____

_____

Congratulate yourself!

Decide what you are going to do next and start the process again on the next page of your journal.

Day 29

My Plan

Today I chose to focus on Tip # ___ because: _____

_____

_____

I will experiment by: _____

_____

_____

Because: _____

_____

_____

Right now, I feel: _____

_____

_____

Do your experiment.

My Results

When I did this experiment, I noticed: _____

_____

_____

_____

Right now, I feel: _____

_____

_____

_____

Congratulate yourself!

Decide what you are going to do next and start the process again on the next page of your journal.

Day 30

My Plan

Today I chose to focus on Tip # __ because: _____

_____

_____

I will experiment by: _____

_____

_____

Because: _____

_____

_____

Right now, I feel: _____

_____

_____

Do your experiment.

My Results

When I did this experiment, I noticed: _____

_____

_____

_____

Right now, I feel: _____

_____

_____

_____

Congratulations! Completing this process for 30 days is an achievement which has set you firmly on the path of creating a partnership relationship. This is a practice you can certainly continue to do for as long as it helps you to focus on achieving your relationship goals.

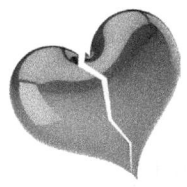

Special Bonus Reminder

If you did not download *How to Both Win the "Yeah But…" Game* when you started to read this book, do it now.

Almost everyone needs help with this because when

- You want to help your partner with a problem.
- You know how to help with the problem.
- Your partner turns away your help.

You need to know how to manage this deadly relationship trap and empower your partner instead. It's easier said than done—until you know how! Claim your copy and learn this important trick right now.

www.BooksByLaurie.com/win

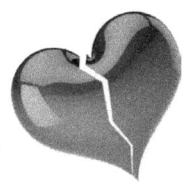

Please Help Me Reach New Readers

Chances are that you checked out the reviews on this book when you purchased it. Reviews are critical to help prospective readers decide to read books. I would be thrilled if you would leave a review NOW, while you are thinking about it.

If you are someone who has done this before, you know how easy it is.

If you're not, you may be shuddering at the memory of grade school book reviews. This is different!!! Really it is!

All you need to do is imagine that you are telling a friend about reading this book. Then follow these steps.

- Say what you would tell your friend into your phone and record it in the notes section and let your phone write it out. (All you need to say is one or two sentences.)
- Email it to yourself.
- Add punctuation if necessary.

Cut and paste your sentences into a review box wherever you buy your books.

I have included a few links to popular places to leave your reviews. Go to www.BooksByLaurie.com or www.Goodreads.com/Laurie_Weiss and click on any book title. Scroll down to find the instructions to leave a review.

I would love to hear from you about how this book impacted you. And, if you have any problems or questions about this book, I would really appreciate hearing from you directly. My email address is Laurie@LaurieWeiss.com. You will find my phone number and social media connections on another page.

Thank you in advance for taking the time to contribute to the conversation about what to read. I truly appreciate it.

Laurie

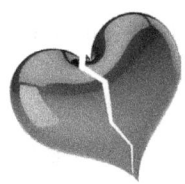

Acknowledgments Relationship Tips for Life Partners: A Personal Story

Once upon a time, when the coaching profession and the Internet were in their infancy and getting email was an exciting adventure, Thomas Leonard, the father of the developing new coaching profession, frequently appeared in my inbox. Thomas pioneered using email to develop a community and his top 10 lists about various topics related to coaching were an unending source of fun and inspiration.

At the same time, my main profession as a psychotherapist was in turmoil because of the general turmoil in the healthcare delivery system. We were rebranding parts of our work as coaching and I had recently published a book on business communication to help me rebrand my practice.

The publishing industry was in turmoil as well and for the first time I needed to assume the responsibility of marketing my new book. Little did I know what a life-changing challenge that would become. I struggled, and used Thomas is my model to learn marketing. Fortunately, I was one of hundreds of people on Thomas's research and development team where he often shared encouragement to "try this on your own."

I had set aside time in my schedule to write about business communication to help market my book and my coaching practice. It was not to be.

That morning I was awakened by a dream of telling my couple clients the same tips over and over again. I couldn't wait to start writing the tips that were pouring out of some part of my being. I wrote tips for couples spontaneously for hours – until my butt froze and my body protested vigorously. I finished the next day!

When no further tips appeared, I looked at my mess, tried to organize it into categories, and decided I needed help. Thomas had just released instructions about how to create your own research and development team and so I chose to experiment with that model. When I asked for help I was astonished at the dozens of sophisticated writers, therapists and coaches who volunteered to participate.

Working with the team provided incredible focus. With their feedback, I refined all these tips and within months the original material was released as a tightly packed print booklet and sold hundreds of copies. Later, each tip was developed further and released as a newsletter and picked up by several very active websites. Eventually that material became an online program, then another book, and led me into a new phase of my career.

It's impossible for me to list and thank everyone who helped. It's been an amazing journey.

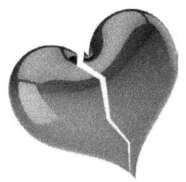

About the Author

Women have been asking Dr. Laurie Weiss questions about relationships for over 45 years. Now she shares her answers to some of them with you.

Relationship Communication Expert, Dr. Laurie Weiss, is internationally known as an expert who helps other relationship consultation professionals develop their skills.

As a psychotherapist, coach, marriage counselor, author and stress-relief expert she has helped more than 60,000 individuals reclaim life energy and find joy in life for more than four decades. She has taught professionals in 13 countries and authored eight books that make complex information accessible to anyone. Her latest, **Letting It Go**, teaches rapid anxiety and stress relief. http://www.Laurie Weiss.com

Dr. Weiss is one of only two Master Certified Logosynthesis Practitioners in the United States. She is a Certified Transactional Analysis Trainer with Clinical and Organizational Specialties and a Master Certified Coach. Her work has been translated into German, Chinese, Spanish, French and Portuguese.

She is passionate about helping people have the important conversations that build great personal and working relationships. She says, "I have an unshakeable belief, based on over 45 years of experience, that people are doing the very best they can with the resources they have available to them at any given moment."

Dr. Laurie and her husband, Dr. Jonathan B. Weiss, started working together in 1970. Both Drs. Weiss love mixing business and pleasure and enjoy visiting professional colleagues and friends around the globe. They live and work in Littleton, CO, USA.

She loves adventures, went indoor skydiving for the first time at age 67 and zip lining for the first time at age 75. She has been blessed by elephants in India, walked on hot coals, visited Camelot, flown over the Pyramids, and spent an afternoon at the sex temples at Khajiraho and learned more possible sex positions than she can possibly remember.

E-mail: Laurie@LaurieWeiss.com

Office: 303-794-5379

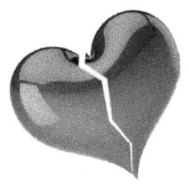

How to Work With Dr. Laurie

My husband, Dr. Jonathan B. Weiss and I have been married since 1960 and business partners since 1972 when we were teaching Transactional Analysis throughout the United States. We have been learning and teaching cutting edge tools for healing and transformation for over 45 years.

We have both been Teaching and Supervising Transactional Analysts for over four decades. Currently we are the only Certified Logosynthesis Practitioners in the United States. Either or both of us would be delighted to help you learn more about creating joy and satisfaction in your life and your important relationships.

Contact Us: We Usually Answer the Phone

Relationship Tips for Life Partners

You can contact us directly to discuss what is best for you and your group. We offer a variety of options including CLASSES, TALKS, BOOK GROUP VISITS, PROFESSIONAL CONFERENCE PRESENTATIONS, TRAINING, INDIVIDUAL and COUPLES APPOINTMENTS. We work with our clients in person, by phone and by Skype.

Dr. Laurie Weiss:

LaurieWeiss@EmpowermentSystems.com

Dr. Jonathan Weiss: Weiss@EmpowermentSystems.com

Empowerment Systems

506 West Davies Way

Littleton, CO 80120 USA

303-794-5379

DR. LAURIE WEISS

Websites

Personal: http://www.LaurieWeiss.com

Logosynthesis: http://www.LogosynthesisColorado.com

Business: http://www.EmpowermentSystems.com

Purchase Books: http://www.BooksbyLaurie.com

Social Media

Facebook: https://www.Facebook.com/laurieweiss

LinkedIn: http://www.Linkedin.com/in/laurieweiss

Pinterest: https://www.Pinterest.com/laurieweiss/

Twitter: https://Twitter.com/@LaurieWeiss

Goodreads: https://www.Goodreads.com/Laurie_Weiss

Blogs

Personal Development: http://www.IDontNeedTherapy.com/blog

Relationship: http://RelationshipHQ.com/blog/

Business Communication: http://www.DareToSayIt.com/blog

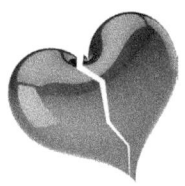

*About the Secrets of
Happy Relationships Series*

Relationships aren't easy. Relationships are often confused and messy with partners trying to find happiness in all the wrong ways.

Real relationships get messy because even though you think your life partner is just like you, he or she isn't. You are two different people trying to meet the challenge of creating and maintaining a happy and loving relationship, perhaps without much useful information.

To make matters worse, you live in the midst of the outmoded role expectations of a culture that values drama and competition and extreme busyness. Most media doesn't help. It focuses on difficult relationships, not successful ones.

Ordinary relationships have their ups and downs and almost nobody writes about those cycles. It's no wonder there are so many misunderstandings. Creating a lasting, loving, growing relationship is an incredible challenge. It's completely natural to have questions about your relationship.

I've been answering questions about relationships since 1973 when I was in newly minted TA (Transactional Analysis) therapist and was sure I had the answers to all the problems of the world. I had been married for 13 years and we had survived some major challenges. I was happily learning and using our new tools. Over four decades later, we are still married, and I've learned a lot.

It's been my pleasure and privilege to help people sort out the misconceptions, misunderstandings and challenges of creating happy, loving relationships. Being happy together is a gift my husband and I have given each other through the work of addressing issues as they arise. It's a gift you can have also; by giving it to each other.

Books in the Secrets of Happy Relationships Series

**Are You My Perfect Partner?
To Marry or Not to Marry …**
Are you really ready to get married?

**Being Married:
Secrets Women Wish They Knew**
*Crucial information you need
to know about marriage*

**Stop Poisoning Your Marriage
with These Common Beliefs**
*Are you letting these myths
undermine your marriage?*

Relationship Tips for Life Partners
Critical guidelines for creating a true partnership

Reconnect to Rescue Your Marriage:
Avoid Divorce and Feel Loved Again
What to do before leaving your troubled marriage

Stop Arguing and Start Talking …
even if you are afraid your only answer is divorce!
Are you ready to have these loving,
productive conversations with your spouse?

Being Happy Together:
What to Do to Keep Love Alive
Unlock secrets to rapid relationship
renewal in just an hour a week

Other Books by Laurie Weiss

Letting It Go: Relieve Anxiety and Toxic
Stress in Just a Few Minutes Using Only Words
(Rapid Relief with Logosynthesis®)
*Are you ready for relaxation to replace
anxiety in your life?*

Emotional Self-Help: I Don't Need Therapy,
But Where Do I Turn for Answers?
Do you need to become emotionally literate?
www.BooksByLaurie.com/answers

Recovery From CoDependency:
It's Never Too Late To Reclaim Your Childhood
Are you ready to release your codependency?
www.BooksByLaurie.com/recovery

**An Action Plan for Your Inner Child:
Parenting Each Other**
Are you ready to reclaim your inner child?
https://www.amazon.com/dp/1558741658

**What Is the Emperor Wearing?
Truth-Telling in Business Relationships**
Do you wish you dared to tell the truth?
www.BooksByLaurie.com/emperor

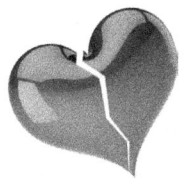

Enjoy this preview of another book in the
Secrets of Happy Relationships series:

Reconnect to Rescue Your Marriage: Avoid Divorce and Feel Loved Again

I've Broken Trust by Withholding Money

You say he wants to end the marriage because he can't trust you, but you want to save the marriage anyhow. I wonder whether he's just reflecting your lack of trust in him back to you. Let me explain. You have admitted withholding money in a separate account, but why would you withhold money if you completely trusted your husband?

Often when one partner in a marriage is afraid to for feeling something that is negative or unacceptable, somehow the other partner expresses the feeling instead. If you really want to reestablish trust and save the marriage, you'll have to start talking about who feels what, and why. This means you will have to look at your own reason for withholding the money in the first place.

Once you understand why you took that action you will need to take responsibility for sharing that with your husband. This is likely to lead to important conversations about your values and his. You have probably made agreements about sharing money in this marriage that you didn't want to make in the first place. If you have wanted to make them, there would've been no reason to break them.

You need to renegotiate those agreements. I know that can be challenging: that's why I included 11 different conversation starters about money for couples in The Being Happy Program. I suggest that you only make agreements that you are willing and intend to keep. If you and your husband can't resolve these issues you must think seriously about whether it makes sense to stay in your marriage.

I can think of all kinds of reasons why a woman would want to keep some money in a separate account. In fact, many couples have clear agreements about how to share some of their money and keep some of the private.

- Many women just want to feel independent and able to spend money in whatever way they choose without needing to account for every penny.

- Sometimes there's a misunderstanding between a husband and wife that leads to one of them feeling threatened because he or she believes that money is going to be used inappropriately.

- Sometimes there's real evidence that one of the partners uses money in a way that's detrimental to the family.

Taking responsibility for negotiating how money is to be handled is a good way to begin to reestablish trust between you and your husband. But even more important is demonstrating your commitment to either keep the agreements that you make or renegotiating them instead of changing them without consulting your partner.

***

You'll find links to all the *Secrets of Happy Relationship Series* books at www.BooksByLaurie.com. Go there now and order the next book you need to create the happy relationship you want and deserve.

www.ingramcontent.com/pod-product-compliance
Lightning Source LLC
Chambersburg PA
CBHW071715020426
42333CB00017B/2280